WEYMOUTH'S SEASIDE HERITAGE

Published by English Heritage, Kemble Drive, Swindon SN2 2GZ
www.english-heritage.org.uk

English Heritage is the Government's statutory advisor on all aspects of the historic environment.

© English Heritage 2008

Printing 10 9 8 7 6 5 4 3 2 1

Images (except as otherwise shown) © English Heritage, © English Heritage.NMR or © Crown copyright.NMR.

First published 2008

ISBN 978 1 84802 008 5
Product code 51429

Weymouth & Portland Borough Council and the South West of England Regional Development Agency
have made a financial contribution towards the publication of this book as part of the Seafront Regeneration
Project.

British Library Cataloguing in Publication Data
A CIP catalogue record for this book is available from the British Library.

Application for the reproduction of images should be made to the National Monuments Record. Every effort has
been made to trace the copyright holders and we apologise in advance for any unintentional omissions, which
we would be pleased to correct in any subsequent edition of this book.

The National Monuments Record is the public archive of English Heritage. For more information, contact NMR
Enquiry and Research Services, National Monuments Record Centre, Kemble Drive, Swindon SN2 2GZ;
telephone (01793) 414600.

Photographs by James O Davies and Peter Williams
Graphics by Nigel Fradgley and Kate Parsons
Brought to publication by René Rodgers, Publishing, English Heritage
Page layout by George Hammond
Printed in the UK by Cambridge Printing

Front cover
The houses to the south side of the
harbour provided much of the
accommodation for Weymouth's first
visitors. This colourful, historic
townscape continues to be an attractive
destination for modern tourists.
[DP054481]

Inside front cover
The Punch and Judy Show on the
beach was run by Professor Guy
Higgins from the mid-1970s until
his retirement in 2005.
[AA036100]

Back Cover
The quayside on the south side of
the harbour now contains many
cafés, restaurants and shops that
have proved popular with visitors
and residents.
[DP054484]

WEYMOUTH'S SEASIDE HERITAGE

Allan Brodie, Colin Ellis, David Stuart and Gary Winter

Contents

Frontispiece
This late 19th-century photograph shows the Esplanade with only a few people about, a consequence of the long exposures needed in Victorian cameras.
[BB87/00002]

Acknowledgements

The historical section of this book is based on fieldwork and research conducted by Allan Brodie, David Stuart and Gary Winter of English Heritage and Colin Ellis of Weymouth & Portland Borough Council. Maureen Attwooll, John Cattell, Colum Giles, Barry Jones and Simon Williams kindly read the manuscript and offered useful comments. The contemporary photographs were taken by James O Davies and Peter Williams, and Mike Hesketh-Roberts undertook the task of making the project team's photographs compatible with the National Monuments Record's systems. The map on the inside back cover was prepared by Kate Parsons; Nigel Fradgley redrew the plans in Fig 23. Other help, in various forms, was provided by numerous staff of the National Monuments Record in Swindon. Elaine Arthurs at STEAM Museum of the Great Western Railway located and supplied the image of holidaymakers boarding the train at Swindon (Fig 35). Charles Wagner kindly allowed us to copy and reproduce Figs 5 and 30. Figs 1 and 2 were provided by the British Library, Weymouth Museum provided a series of historic images of the town (Figs 8, 12, 13 and 17) and Watkins Dally Landscape Architects supplied Figs 67 and 68. While every effort has been made to trace copyright holders of other images, we apologise to any who we have not been able to contact. The extract on p 1 is Copyright © Paul Theroux, 1983.

During our numerous visits we have been consistently and enthusiastically welcomed and helped by many people who live and work in Weymouth and Portland. In particular we would like to express our sincere thanks to the staff and volunteers at Weymouth Library, Dorset History Centre, Weymouth Museum and Portland Museum.

Foreword

The seaside is part of the national psyche. It is part of our past as a seafaring nation, but it is also a place of fond childhood memories. In the past 250 years, our seaside towns responded to a growing demand for holidays and they developed their own distinctive character. However, during the last half-century cheaper travel has taken many English holidaymakers abroad and this has led to economic problems and physical decline in many resorts. An English Heritage survey in 2007 found that 75 per cent of people believed that 'many seaside towns are shabby and run down'.

However, a similar percentage felt that 'the historic character of seaside towns is what makes them beautiful and enjoyable' and an appreciation of this historic character will be at the heart of revitalising seaside resorts. This book describes the colourful history of the seaside holiday at Weymouth, one of England's first seaside resorts, and it examines the buildings that survive to tell this story. It also demonstrates how the historic environment can be an important part of the future of the town. Well-maintained historic buildings are not only a key attraction for modern visitors; they also contribute to making a town a pleasant place in which to live and work.

Although 250 years separate the Georgian sea bather from the modern sunbather, the lure of Weymouth's wide bay, sandy beach and stunning seafront still proves irresistible. Weymouth is well placed to revive its fortunes as a resort, but there will, inevitably, be changes. English Heritage, Weymouth & Portland Borough Council, and the South West of England Regional Development Agency have different roles to play in this revival, but all are concerned that a well-presented historic environment should play a central part in the future of the town and its economic regeneration.

Lord Bruce-Lockhart, Chairman of English Heritage

Councillor Doug Hollins, Environment Briefholder,
and Historic Environment and Design Champion,
Weymouth & Portland Borough Council

Jane Henderson, Chief Executive of South West of England
Regional Development Agency

CHAPTER 1

Introduction

I liked Weymouth immediately. It was grand without being pompous. It had a real harbour. It was full of boats. All its architecture was intact, the late-Georgian terraces facing the esplanade and the sea, and cottages and old warehouses on the harbour. I liked the look of the houses, their elegance, and the smell of fish and beer among them. I walked around. There was plenty of space. The weather was perfect. I thought: I could live here.[1]

In 1982 Paul Theroux took a farewell tour of Britain by travelling around its coast. He found many things of interest and amusement on his journey, but Weymouth was a place where he felt he could live. So why Weymouth?

Its perceived healthy situation and picturesque, wide, sandy bay led enthusiastic guidebook writers in the 19th century to liken it to Montpellier or Naples, but Weymouth also has many other charms. It has an almost unbroken line of elegant seafront terraces, built for new residents and for the visitors who arrived in increasing numbers during the 18th and 19th centuries. These houses chart Weymouth's seaside history, from the haphazard, small-scale developments of the mid- to late 18th century through to the confident, long terraces of the first half of the 19th century. But Weymouth is more than just its seafront. It has the tightly knit old town, with some buildings dating back to before the Civil War, and at its heart, both in terms of its geography and history, lies the harbour with a colourful array of working boats and pleasure craft.

Weymouth grew rapidly as a result of tourism and it is still a popular summer destination for thousands of visitors; however, since the 1970s, as in other resorts, their numbers have declined. The town had another major source of income – the numerous defence establishments clustered around the Isle of Portland – but cutbacks in the past 15 years have also seen this source of employment diminish significantly.

However, as well as difficulties, there have been new opportunities to boost the local economy. Weymouth lies at the heart of the 'Dorset and East Devon Coast', which was inscribed as a World Heritage Site in 2001, and in 2005 the successful bid for the London 2012 Olympic and Paralympic Games included the Weymouth & Portland National Sailing Academy as the venue for the sailing competitions.

The sweeping bay of Weymouth – seen from Greenhill in the north of the town – shows the long beach and its seafront terraces. [DP055511]

While these will bring some short-term, and longer-term, prosperity to Weymouth, its natural and built assets could be put to better service for the town. Like all seaside resorts Weymouth suffers from seasonality, yet visitors flock to inland historic towns all year round. There is still a perception that once the warm summer days are over, seaside resorts are no longer obvious destinations for a visit. Some resorts make specific offers to attract more visitors out of season: Blackpool tries to stretch its season by offering the illuminations through September and October, and other resorts, such as Bournemouth, offer conference facilities to attract people on business trips all year round. St Ives has built on its international reputation as an art colony and Newquay can attract hardy surfing visitors, often regardless of the weather. Whitstable is a magnet for lovers of oysters and seafood throughout the months with an 'R' in them – the long winter months.

Weymouth has already begun to use its natural attractions to bring visitors throughout the year, with large numbers of sailors, birdwatchers and walkers coming during the traditional closed season. However, its other charms could also provide a way of catching the eye of the increasingly affluent weekend and short-break market. Weymouth can offer a special holiday in one of England's most attractive historic towns; a town that also has the sea, fresh sea air and beautiful sands to offer. With the right mixture of hotels, restaurants and attractions, holidaymakers could be drawn to Weymouth throughout the year. However, a successful resort also has to be a good place to live, with well-paid, full-time jobs as well as the lower-paid, often seasonal, jobs that are a key feature of the tourist industry.

People once came to seaside resorts in search of improved health, the novel and the exotic, and while these themes still have a role today, there is a growing recognition that a stimulating and well-maintained historic environment can be a major attraction for visitors and a driver for regeneration. English Heritage believes that if the heritage of a town is to survive, it will have to work for its living, and that this can be achieved by positive reuse of historic buildings and sensitive restoration. People want to stay or dine in places with character and new media-related businesses can also thrive in the intimate environment of a fine historic town. There will be a demand for new, large-scale developments to meet some of the needs of residents and visitors, but these need to harmonise with the existing fabric of the town, not through poor-quality pastiche, but by sensitive, high-quality design.

Growing concern about climate change and excessive exposure to the sun has already led some people to reconsider holidaying abroad and look again at the English seaside as a holiday destination. By adding other strands to the attractions of a town, seaside resorts can prosper in the future. Weymouth has a colourful past, including over 250 years of seaside holidays. Celebrating this past can become an important part of Weymouth's future.

CHAPTER 2

Weymouth and Melcombe Regis prior to 1748

In the Middle Ages, Weymouth consisted of two distinct settlements each with their own local government and Members of Parliament. Weymouth was the name of the older settlement on the south side of the harbour, while the larger town, on the north side, was Melcombe Regis.

Weymouth was first mentioned in the 10th century and by the 11th century the ports of Weymouth and Melcombe Regis were being referred to in documents. In 1280 Edward I granted a Charter of Incorporation to Melcombe Regis and its regular grid pattern, reminiscent of planned towns such as New Buckenham or Winchelsea, was laid out. In July 1348 the Black Death was reputedly introduced into England through Melcombe Regis and two centuries later John Leland remarked that it 'hath beene far bigger then it is now', though he attributed its reduced size to French attacks rather than the plague.[2]

Until the 18th century, both settlements – despite their proximity to the sea – were orientated to the river and the safe harbour that separated them, as trade and shipping were the mainstays of the economy. However, a Dominican friary, established in 1418, was granted a large area of land on the shore and the friars built a jetty that appears on a late 16th-century map. This modest structure, approximately on the site of Alexandra Gardens, marked the first eastward extension of Melcombe Regis, a process that continued through the construction of increasingly substantial piers and embankments into the 19th and 20th centuries.

The earliest depiction of the town shows Melcombe Regis as a circular island linked to the mainland by a long, narrow causeway, presumably a sandbank topped by a road (Fig 1). Two towns sharing a harbour led to a series of heated, sometimes violent disputes. Thomas Gerard, writing in the 1620s, says that 'having wearied the Lordes of the Councill and other Courts, with their contentious Importunities … they were by Acte of Parliament … incorporated into one Bodie' in 1571.[3] While the town was still formally called Weymouth and Melcombe Regis, it was increasingly referred to as Weymouth only. The most tangible symbol of unification was the erection of the first bridge across the harbour in 1593–7. Prior to this the harbour had to be crossed by a small ferry boat, an experience that can still be enjoyed by visitors during the summer.

This modern aerial photograph shows the key features of the town – its river, harbour and long sandy beach.
[NMR 21660/05]

A late 16th-century map in the British Library shows Weymouth and Melcombe Regis just prior to the construction of the first bridge (Fig 2). Weymouth was a long, narrow settlement based around its High Street and along the riverside. Hope Cove (on the south bank of the river in Fig 2) was depicted as a sandy inlet with a few houses clinging to its southern side and there was a crescent-shaped line of houses facing the sea at Newton's Cove (below and to the right of Hope Cove). Melcombe Regis was bounded by the river in the south and the west. To the east a narrow strip of grassland separated the town from the beach and at the north end of the town the 'Conybery hills' formed the boundary. These three 'hills', on the site of Bond Street and Lower Bond Street, were small banks with gaps between them in line with St Thomas and St Mary Streets. To the north of the banks was sandy grassland, the type of land enjoyed by rabbits, and to the north-west of the town was the 'Great Barow', presumably a prehistoric burial mound. At the north-east corner of the town, on the seafront, there was a 'Smal Platforme', designed to protect the town from seaborne attack.

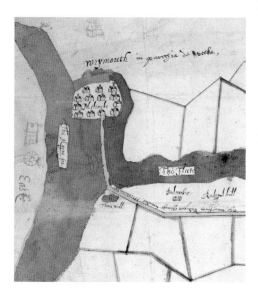

Figure 1
This mid-16th-century map in a manuscript is schematic, but it does indicate how people thought of the two towns, with Melcombe Regis almost as an island distinct from Weymouth across the river. [©British Library Board. All rights reserved (Cotton MS Augustus i.ii.22)]

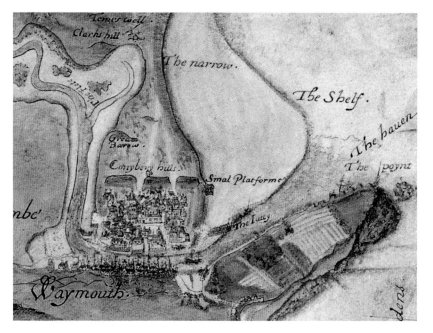

Figure 2
This map, showing the area in greater detail, illustrates how the town was orientated to the river, the seafront of Melcombe Regis still being undeveloped. The Conybery Hills to the north seem to be defensive, but their name suggests they were rabbit warrens. [©British Library Board. All rights reserved (Cotton MS Augustus i.i.32)]

Figure 3 (below, left)
This famous house at the corner of Maiden Street and St Edmund Street, with the embedded cannon ball in its gable, shows how the town's houses suffered in the mid-17th century.
[DP024376]

Figure 4 (below, right)
This house, at 16–17 Trinity Street, may have once been covered with thatch and would have resembled some of the houses that can be seen in villages around the town. This building was used as the assembly rooms before the new extension was built behind it (see Fig 26).
[DP054518]

During the Civil War, both sides of the river suffered considerable damage and any early, timber-framed houses would have been particularly vulnerable to the effects of warfare (Fig 3) as well as the periodic fires that occurred, including the 1665 fire that destroyed 37 houses. By the early 18th century, Weymouth was probably an eclectic mix of old timber-framed buildings and more recent, stone buildings with mullioned windows. Some of this latter type of house survive on both sides of the river and, although they are now covered in slate or tile, most were originally roofed with stone slabs or thatch (Fig 4). Thatched roofs were a common sight until 1784 when the provisions of the 1776 Improvement Act came into force requiring the removal of all existing thatched roof coverings.

The last account of the town before sea bathing became a popular pursuit was provided by Daniel Defoe who visited in the 1720s. He said that: 'Weymouth is a sweet, clean, agreeable Town, considering its low Situation, and close to the Sea; 'tis well built, and has a great many good substantial Merchants in it; who drive a considerable Trade, and have a good Number of Ships belonging to the Town'[4] (Fig 5).

Sea bathing at Weymouth

From the late 17th century onwards, there is growing evidence of a new interest in seawater as a medical treatment and by the 1730s a number of small coastal towns were playing host to wealthy visitors wishing to bathe in the sea. Margate, Hastings and Brighton were small ports with uncertain economic futures until this new tourist phenomenon emerged. The existing homes of merchants and fishermen, and the primitive entertainment facilities of these towns, were soon welcoming the highest strata of English society fresh from their homes and lodgings in London or Bath, or their country seats.

The first reference to sea bathing at Weymouth dates from 1748: 'R. Prowse and Jos. Bennet had twenty-one year leases granted to them, so that they might erect two wooden bathing houses on the N. side of the Harbour.'[5] This has been interpreted to be permission to build bathing machines, but as mobile structures, would their location have been specified? At Margate and Ramsgate 'bathing houses' were for people waiting for a bathing machine, though the first definite reference to these institutions at Margate only dates from the 1750s. Reinhold Rücker Angerstein, the Swedish industrialist and spy, visited England in the mid-1750s and described the scene he witnessed:

> The bay of the sea that lies east of Weymouth has a very clayey bottom, uncomfortable for persons who might wish to take cold baths. Wagons have therefore been constructed carrying huts made of boards, capable of carrying seven or eight people, who are driven out into the water, where they can enter the sea by means of steps and get out again, without being crowded or seen from the shore. This costs 1 shilling per person.[6]

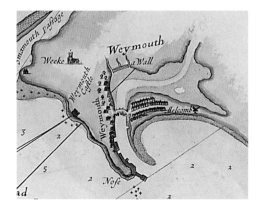

Figure 5
Though Defoe visited in the 1720s, the Weymouth he saw must have been very similar to the town depicted on Greenville Collins' chart, which was surveyed in the 1680s. By that date the town seems to have expanded north of its medieval boundaries and a bridge now linked the two settlements.
[Image courtesy of Charles Wagner; DP054545]

The most unusual feature of this description is the size of the 'huts' described. Typical 18th-century bathing machines were designed for one, or perhaps two bathers, though by the late 19th century larger, multiple-occupancy saloons were employed at a number of resorts, including Weymouth. Perhaps the size of the bathing huts was the reason that their location was specified in 1748? Irrespective of their precise function, the willingness to make a significant investment in bathing facilities suggests the presence of a fairly mature bathing culture.

Weymouth's success as a resort was guaranteed when it began to attract wealthy and powerful patrons. The first celebrity to make frequent visits was Ralph Allen, who made a fortune from the postal service and later through having a near monopoly in the provision of building stone in rapidly expanding Bath. Allen first came to Weymouth in 1750 and thereafter returned annually until his death in 1764 (Fig 6). Allen's interest in bathing is further demonstrated by his construction of a cold-water bath at Prior Park, his grand estate overlooking Bath.

Prince William Henry, Duke of Gloucester, first visited Weymouth in 1765 and by the early 1780s he had built a house on the seafront known as Gloucester Lodge, a grand building that became an end-of-terrace house that would prove fit for a king. In 1788 George III was struck down with porphyria, a disease affecting his nervous system, and it was felt that a stay at the seaside would be beneficial. He arrived in Weymouth on 30 June 1789 and stayed for 10 weeks. A week after his arrival he bathed in the sea, an event accompanied by great ceremonials: 'The King bathes, and with great success; a machine follows the Royal one into the sea, filled with fiddlers, who play *God Save the King*, as his majesty takes his plunge.'[7]

During this visit, and subsequent ones, the king and the royal family were at the heart of the social scene, a fact testified by the frequent descriptions of their activities in diaries and in regular reports in *The Times*. As well as a range of semi-official duties, the king attended events at the assembly room at the Royal Hotel or promenaded along the seafront, an activity that often attracted significant crowds. The king also visited local aristocrats in their country seats; he regularly inspected regiments of troops in barracks or camps near Weymouth and he went on board naval ships moored offshore. The royal presence, and the consequent military occupation of buildings and camps in and around

Figure 6
2 & 2A Trinity Road was the house where Ralph Allen is reputed to have stayed when he visited Weymouth. However, the existing building seems to date from later in the 18th century and it was raised by a storey in the late 19th century.
[AA042018]

Weymouth, helped to make the town lively at a period when war with France could have discouraged some visitors from venturing to the south coast (Fig 7).

From 1791 to 1802 the king visited Weymouth every summer, except 1793, and in 1801 he bought Gloucester Lodge from his brother (Fig 8). In 1802 the town council decided to commemorate the king's visits, but it took until 1810 for his statue to be completed (Fig 9). On his death in 1820, Royal Lodge, as it was then known, and its contents were sold (Fig 10). In the sale catalogue, the house was described as consisting of a hall and staff rooms on the ground floor, six 'airy and cheerful Rooms of good Proportions' along with a waiting room and WC on the first floor, ten main rooms and WCs on the second floor and thirteen staff bedchambers in the attic.[8]

Rich patrons demanded facilities and Weymouth was quick to seize the opportunity to entertain and accommodate in style. Between Ralph Allen's

first visit in 1750 and George III's last visit in 1805, the town had begun its transformation from a small working port into a fashionable watering place, suitable for the aristocrats who came as a result of the presence of the royal family. A late 18th-century guidebook mused, proudly, that: 'It is indeed astonishing, that a place which a few years since consisted of very little else than a knot of fisherman's [sic] huts, should in so short a space have undergone such an amazing change, as now to be the first watering place in the kingdom, honoured by the Royal Family, and continued influx of visitors.'[9] Guidebooks were positive about the changes, but the ever irascible John Byng, later Viscount Torrington, said that, as a result of the Duke of Gloucester having built his house, 'Weymouth … is become the resort of the giddy and gay; where the Irish beau, the gouty peer, and the genteel shopkeeper, blend in folly and fine breeding'.[10]

Conventional bathing machines were available at Weymouth by 1774, when five horse-drawn examples were shown on John Hutchins' map (Fig 11). By 1800 over 30 bathing machines could be hired and by 1815 there were more than 40. The most famous bathing machine was the one used by George III. He was provided with a tall machine that was octagonal in plan with large wheels. It bore the royal arms above the door at the rear of the machine.

Bathing machines with modesty hoods offered some privacy and protection, but greater comfort could be enjoyed by visiting a bathhouse. By the end of the 18th century, there were baths on the quay, on the site of the current Royal Dorset Yacht Club. George Carey said that the baths had been built at a cost of £500 to cater for George III, but he took one dip, paid five guineas and refused to return as he said there was not enough salt in the water! A guidebook of the early 1800s stated that: 'These Bathes are lately much improved, by having Marble Troughs, instead of Stone.'[11] By 1836 this bathhouse included four hot baths and eight dressing rooms, suggesting a fairly substantial institution. However, it was superseded in 1842 by the larger Royal Baths, which were located between St Mary Street and St Thomas Street (Fig 12).

The Royal Baths were for the general public, albeit fairly prosperous bathers, but Weymouth also had another, more exclusive bathhouse. A floating bath, for use by the royal family, was moored beside the pier (Fig 13). Inside the hull there were three small pools, the largest one reserved for the king, and

The *grateful* Inhabitants To GEORGE THE THIRD

Figure 9
After a number of years of discussion, the statue of George III was finally unveiled in 1810, five years after the king's last visit to the town. This photo was taken after its restoration in 2008. Another belated commemoration of his visits was a white horse ridden by the king, carved into the hillside at Osmington in 1808. [DP058192]

Figure 10
After the sale of the Royal Lodge (originally Gloucester Lodge), parts of the building (seen on the right side) were later incorporated into the Gloucester Hotel. The hotel was severely damaged by fire in 1927 and during the subsequent rebuilding it was raised by a storey. [DP055554]

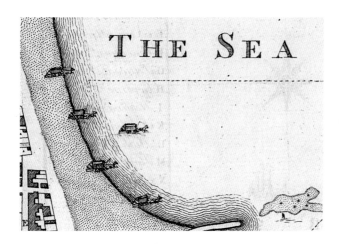

Figure 11
This detail from a map of Weymouth in John Hutchins' The History and Antiquities of the County of Dorset *(1774) shows bathing machines with modesty hoods, a feature introduced by Benjamin Beale at Margate in the 1750s. These allowed visitors to dip in the sea free from public view and protected from waves or strong gusts of wind.*
[DP022292]

Figure 12
Each façade of the Royal Baths had a central door leading into a corridor that ran through the building. The baths and changing rooms were on either side of this passage.
[Weymouth Museum]

Figure 13
George III famously bathed in the sea in 1789
accompanied by a band. However, once he was a
regular visitor to Weymouth, this floating bath
within the hull of a boat was created c 1800.
[Weymouth Museum]

Figure 14
The Spa House at Nottington is three-storied and octagonal in plan with simplified, panelled pilasters at the eight corners. The basement contained the well and baths, and there was a pump room on the ground floor where visitors could drink water, read papers and enjoy convivial company. Sitting rooms and bedrooms occupied the top two floors. [DP055564]

around the baths were dressing rooms. Was the creation of this strange structure a response to George III's complaint about the saltiness of his bath water?

As well as seawater, visitors could enjoy the therapeutic benefits of spring water at two nearby spas. The spring at Nottington had been known since *c* 1720 and in 1830 a new bathhouse was built (Fig 14): 'Mr Thomas Shore, the Proprietor of the Spring, he having at a considerable expence [*sic*], erected *an elegant and spacious SPA HOUSE*, at Nottington, combining a spacious pump

Room, appropriate Warm, Cold, Vapour, and Shower Baths; with suitably connected apartments, and also an excellent Boarding and Lodging House.'[12] Another spring was 'rediscovered' at Radipole in the 1790s and a spa was built to exploit it in 1830. It had a central, octagonal building with two short, flanking wings. Like Nottington, it proved to be a popular destination for trips out from Weymouth.

Although sea bathing practices changed during the 19th century and more people headed for the coast simply for entertainment, health still remained a significant concern at many resorts, through the establishment of bathhouses, hydropathic hotels (where disorders were treated through the use of water) and convalescent homes. A map of 1857 in Weymouth Library shows a hydropathic bathhouse either in or behind Victoria Villa, at the junction of Lennox Street and Victoria Street. A sanatorium was established in 1848 with seven beds for women and children, and in 1862–3 a new building costing £2,000 was built on the corner of Belle Vue and Clarence Buildings (Fig 15).

Figure 15
The sanatorium, a substantial Italianate building, was designed to look like a private dwelling, with the intention that each patient should have their own bedroom. The building was the home of the local authority from 1904 until 1971 and it is now holiday flats.
[DP058194]

Accommodation for visitors

The size of the town in 1774 was only a little larger than it had been in the late 16th century (Fig 16). A small area had been developed to the north of the former Conybery Hills, and although some new houses had been built within the footprint of the original town, most of the early visitors had to find accommodation in relatively small, old houses. Viscount Torrington voiced his feelings about having to stay in older houses in the town in 1782: 'That the infirm, and the upstart, should resort to these fishing holes, may perhaps be accounted for; but that the healthy owners of parks, good houses and good beds, should quit them for confinement, dirt, and misery, appears to me to be downright madness!'[13]

Hutchins' map shows no signs of new developments orientated to exploit their seaside location. Much of the seafront on the Melcombe Regis side was still formed by the rear gardens of buildings located on modern-day New Street and East Street, but within a few years the rapid transformation of the town was under way. One of Weymouth's early guidebooks wrote that 'the

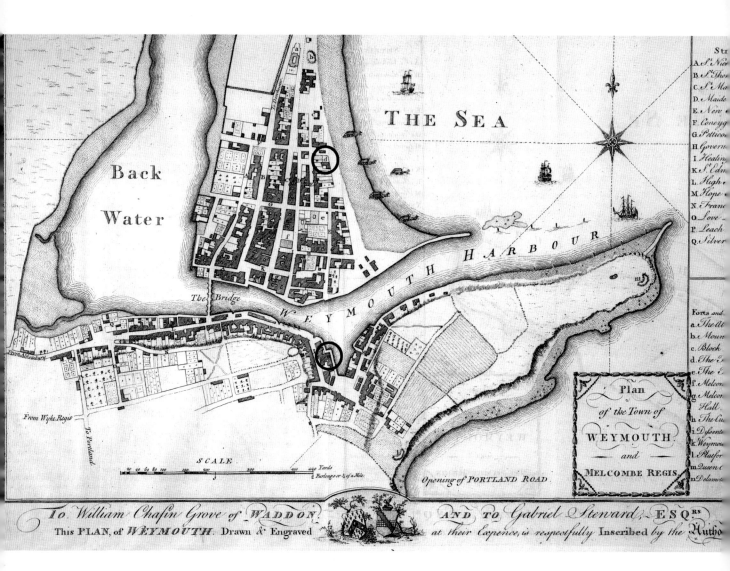

The text visible on the map includes:

THE SEA

Back Water

WEYMOUTH HARBOUR

The Bridge

From Wyke Regis

To Portland

SCALE

Opening of PORTLAND ROAD

Plan of the Town of WEYMOUTH and MELCOMBE REGIS

To William Chafin Grove of WADDON AND TO Gabriel Steward, ESQ.rs This PLAN, of WEYMOUTH. Drawn & Engraved at their Expence, is respectfully Inscribed by the Author

inhabitants by such an influx of money have been encouraged to rebuild, repair, and greatly enlarge the town, which in little more than twenty years has undergone a considerable transformation'.[14]

In the 1770s there were numerous complaints about the lack of decent accommodation, prompting Andrew Sproule, a developer from Bath, to build the Royal Hotel on waste ground to the north of Melcombe Regis, the site now occupied by the present Royal Hotel (Fig 17). Rooms were also available in inns in the town, but the vast majority of visitors stayed in houses that served as

Figure 16
Hutchins' detailed map of 1774 shows the town before the presence of visitors transformed the seafront. The theatre on the seafront (labelled d) and the assembly room at the Old Rooms Inn (n) were the only attractions specifically created for visitors.
[DP022292]

Figure 17
The Royal Hotel was one of the first purpose-built
hotels for visitors to a seaside resort. The hotel offered
separate rooms for families or small groups, with
contiguous dining rooms and bedrooms.
[Weymouth Museum]

lodgings. In 1800 *Ryall's Guidebook* stated that there were many excellent lodging houses in the interior of the town, but by then the most desirable accommodation was on the seafront.

Soon after Sproule built the Royal Hotel and Hutchins' map was published, the first developments began to appear on the seafront, influenced by the interest in sea bathing (Fig 18). An early guidebook recorded that: 'In little more than twenty years we behold this town enlarged by a vast number of elegant buildings. The Esplanade, which even boys remember to have been nothing but a place where the inhabitants deposited all the rubbish of the town, is in no short space converted into one of the most charming promenades in England.'[15]

At the southern end of the seafront the new developments were relatively short terraces, built on the formerly undeveloped sandy land at the rear of the plots of buildings on New Street and East Street. The first terrace, York Buildings, was originally seven houses long (Fig 19). Built in the mid-1780s, it was supplemented by other short terraces at the south end of the Esplanade in the 1790s. However, on the untouched land to the north of Melcombe Regis, longer, taller terraces were constructed (Fig 20), beginning in the 1780s with Gloucester Row, to the north of Gloucester Lodge, and culminating in the 1850s with Victoria Terrace. On land reclaimed at the beginning of the 19th century, Pulteney Buildings and Devonshire Buildings were constructed, extending the Esplanade to the east (Fig 21).

There was also a clear progression in the design of seafront terraces. The earliest terrace – York Buildings – was unadorned by balconies, with a large Venetian window lighting the first floor, but by the 1790s new terraces had balconies in this position. At the start of the 19th century some of the most prominent new developments, such as Pulteney Buildings, Devonshire Buildings and Johnstone Row favoured bow windows rising through two or three stories. This new fashion did not wholly replace balconies, as Belvidere (Fig 22), which took over 30 years to build between 1818 and the 1850s, still employed them. However, during the 1820s and 1830s curved bow windows were favoured at Brunswick Buildings, Frederick Place and Waterloo Place, though the last of the grand seafront terraces, Victoria Terrace, employed balconies in its houses and the standard, mid-19th century canted bay window for rooms in the central hotel.

Figure 18 (top left)
By the time J Crane created this view in 1789, the
first terraces on the seafront had been built.
Gloucester Lodge and the adjacent terrace, which
included the Royal Hotel, were the only major
developments north of the historic town.
[AA050895]

Figure 19 (bottom left)
York Buildings, to the right of the circulating library,
was the first seafront terraced house development.
Although it consisted of three-storied houses, they
were smaller than the houses in later terraces.
[DP055555]

Figure 20 (right)
Royal Terrace – one of the longer, taller terraces – was
built on part of the gardens of Gloucester Lodge. Each
house has three principal storeys plus a basement
and attic and is one room wide and two deep.
[AA036109]

Figure 21
Devonshire Buildings is one of the terraces where
the local authority has been able to enforce a level
of uniformity in the finish of the exterior, in
marked contrast to Royal Terrace (see Fig 20)
where every house is different.
[DP054504]

Apart from Victoria Terrace, these new seafront terraces were wholly composed of conventional houses, usually with single rooms at the front of the block with a similar-sized room behind. The stairs were predominantly at the rear of the buildings, though in Johnstone Row they were between the front and rear rooms. On the upper floors, the plan would have been similar to the ground floor, but additional rooms may have been created by using the space above the entrance hall or by some limited subdivision of the large rooms. Although houses in plan and appearance, they were not usually used as conventional houses. These provided the lodgings required for the growing

Figure 22
Belvidere looks like a unified terrace, but a map of 1819 shows that the four central houses were built before the other houses in the terrace.
[DP054515]

No.4 Royal Terrace   No.8 Frederick Place   No.7 Belvidere

No.4 Brunswick Terrace

No.2 Johnstone Row

Waterloo Place

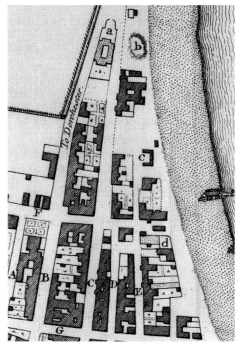

Figure 23 (above, left)
Seaside houses employed the types of plan found in
towns throughout England, but instead of being
family homes with definite functions for each room,
these were used flexibly to accommodate visitors.

Figure 24 (above, right)
On Hutchins' 1774 map Block House Fort (labelled c)
and Mount Joy Fort (b) were probably nearing the
end of their usefulness and had certainly ceased
to be used by c 1800; New Street is labelled as E.
The interruption to the line of the Esplanade at the
lower-right corner of the map is the probable site of
the 'Smal Platforme' seen in Fig 2.
[DP022292]

numbers of visitors who were seeking greater comfort than they would have enjoyed in older houses in the town (Fig 23). Early guidebooks to Weymouth reveal that almost every house in the new seafront terraces provided lodgings. In *c* 1800 there were 105 houses offering lodgings and 184 houses provided visitors with accommodation by 1836. The standard arrangement seems to have been for guests to buy their food for their landlord or landlady to cook, though they were also supplied with some basic, household items as part of their rent. Wealthy families might be able to rent a whole house, but more often the pressure on accommodation during the summer meant that most lodgers would have had to make do with a floor or even just a room.

The forts that once existed on the seafront had a small, but noticeable, effect on the later arrangement of the terraces on the Esplanade. Between York Buildings and Johnstone Row there is a clear interruption in the line of the new seafront terraces. This is partly to link New Street to the Esplanade, but it seems to have also been influenced by the presence of some remains of the Block House Fort. The fort was shown on Hutchins' map of 1774 (Fig 24) though it does not appear on a *c* 1800 map, despite the potentially greater need for some defences from a possible French attack. If the late 16th-century map of Weymouth and Melcombe Regis (*see* Fig 2) was reliable, the location of another military structure – the 'Smal Platforme' – also seems to have influenced the arrangement of later buildings. It may have been where East Street joins the Esplanade and this may explain the change of alignment in the buildings on the seafront and the gap at this location on the 1774 map.

Figure 25
Harvey's Library was divided into two parts by a courtyard, with the library and card room in the front range facing the sea with the more domestic rooms in the rear block. [AA037420]

Entertaining Georgian visitors

If the improvement of health was ostensibly the *raison d'être* of seaside resorts, this concern was quickly supplemented, and later overtaken, by the desire to be entertained. However, there was always a fine balance to be struck between improving health through sea bathing and making sure that the benefits were not undone by the effects of the accompanying busy social whirl. In the 18th century medical writers were insistent that bathing should take place in the morning before any food was consumed and bathing machines usually only operated between 6am and midday. This left the rest of the day for leisure and society. After a hearty breakfast, visitors threw themselves into the hectic social scene regulated by the town's Master of Ceremonies. As in spa towns, the heart of this activity was dominated by three formal institutions: the circulating library, the assembly rooms and the theatre.

The circulating library was usually the social centre of a resort during the day, but its range of activities belied the rather fusty image suggested by the name. It offered a place for people to congregate and socialise; books could be borrowed; newspapers could be read; and tea could be drunk. A list of the lodgings available in the resort was usually maintained by the librarian and there was often a register recording the notable visitors staying in the town. There were also card rooms where gentlemen could squander their inheritances and within the library there were opportunities to purchase jewellery, stationery and a wide variety of fancy goods.

Harvey's Library was located on the Esplanade between Charlotte Row and York Buildings (Fig 25). Physical evidence suggests that it predates the two flanking terraces and therefore probably dates from the early 1780s. One early guidebook described the library:

The principal Library is built in a very elegant style, delightfully situated about the center of the Esplanade; where there is a commodious room to read the Newspapers, &c. with every suitable accommodation to make it agreeable to the Nobility and Gentry who continually resort to it. The Card Room over the Library is 45 feet long, 23 wide, and 16 feet wide, and is very handsomely furnished. It may not be presumptious [*sic*] to say that it deserves to be ranked among the first Libraries in the Kingdom.[16]

Harvey's Library faced competition from a nearby rival. A map of around 1800 shows Wood's Library a few doors to the south; by 1836 it was known as Commins' Library. A bookplate inside copies of Commins' own guidebook held in the Weymouth Library and the British Library shows that it was located in a three-storied building with an attic, a standard house converted to serve as a library. Circulating libraries were fragile enterprises, changing hands frequently and regularly going out of business, and at different times there were also libraries in St Mary Street, St Thomas Street and in a building opposite the statue of George III.

Wealthy visitors also turned to the assembly rooms for entertainment and the company of fellow socialites during the day and for formal assemblies during the evening. Weymouth had acquired an assembly room by the early 1770s, on the south side of the harbour, at the rear of a 16th-century building on Trinity Street (Fig 26). This had closed by 1785 due to the success of the new assembly room in the Royal Hotel in Gloucester Row on the Esplanade. The new assembly room was 70ft long and 40ft wide (21m by 12m), and the hotel also provided a coffee room, a billiard room, a card room and shops. In 1836 the 'Ball Room' was described as 'spacious, lofty, and very handsomely fitted up; one hundred couples can dance in it with the greatest ease'.[17]

Aspiring resorts also required a theatre. In some towns these began as makeshift facilities, with performances sometimes being held in a barn, but once the number of visitors had grown, a purpose-built facility became viable. In Weymouth the first performance at what was later known as the Theatre Royal was on 8 July 1771, meaning that it was one of the first, purpose-built theatres outside London. Its location on the seafront, near where Bond Street joins the Esplanade, is marked on the 1774 map (*see* Fig 16). It was consistently

Figure 26
Weymouth's first purpose-built assembly room
was located near Ralph Allen's house. This simple,
two-storied brick building survives as the Old
Rooms Inn. The early building to which it was
attached is illustrated in Fig 4.
[DP022313]

described in early guidebooks as being small. Fanny Burney, accompanying the king and queen to the theatre in 1789, found that: ''Tis a pretty little theatre, but its entertainment was quite in the barn style: a mere medley – songs, dances, imitations – and all very bad.'[18] George Carey, who appears to have been as cantankerous as Viscount Torrington, described the theatre as being 'on a contracted scale, built in the shape of a wig-box, and not much wider' and he was equally dismissive of the performers who appeared there, saying that 'the performers are generally of a moderate description, only fit to make the audience laugh, by putting nature out of joint'.[19]

The theatre had a capacity of around 300–400, with the entrance to the boxes in Augusta Place and the entrance to the pit and gallery in New Street. Externally it had a three-storied façade on the Esplanade, with large shop windows on the ground floor flanking a central entrance. The auditorium was U-shaped with one or possibly two tiers of boxes and a gallery running around the central pit, which was set beneath the level of the stage. The last performance in the theatre took place on 4 December 1859.

As well as formal entertainment institutions, people visited coffee houses and taverns; they also promenaded along the seafront and spent time on the beach, making sandcastles, or collecting seashells and other types of flora or fauna. Guidebooks also refer to regattas and race meetings; trips out to sea were also popular, small pleasure boats being available at the end of the pier. Substantial sections of guidebooks were devoted to nearby places that visitors could ride out to, including the Isle of Portland and Lulworth Cove. Abigail Gawthern recorded in her diary that during her holiday in Weymouth in June 1805 her husband Frank took a boat trip to the wreck of the *Abergavenny* and visited the lighthouses on Portland.[20]

Georgian and Victorian guidebooks also placed considerable emphasis on religious worship and consequently the charms, and sometimes the facilities, of churches and chapels were described, much as the more obvious forms of 'entertainment' were documented (Fig 27). Irreligious pursuits were also present in Georgian resorts, though in at least one commentator's case not in sufficient quantity. Rather predictably, Viscount Torrington wrote that: 'I begin to be heartily tired of this place, for it is all sameness and dullness: a gentleman left it some days since, saying he would not stay in any place, where were neither wenching, drinking, or gaming; and neither of the three are practised here.'[21]

Figure 27
St Mary's Church was the main church of Melcombe Regis and was rebuilt in 1817. In guidebooks its main attraction was a painting of the The Last Supper *by Sir James Thornhill. It was presented to the town in 1721, the year before he became one of Weymouth's MPs. [DP024378]*

The harbour in Georgian and Victorian Weymouth

Although the income from visitors was of growing importance from the late 18th century onwards, the harbour still lay at the heart of Weymouth's economy and identity. The north side of the harbour – the Melcombe Regis

Figure 28
Included among the buildings that line the north side of the harbour is the former Custom House, an ordinary house later converted to this use. Beside it, the warehouse has been converted into a visitor attraction. [AA036113]

side – contains the main working buildings of the harbour, including the old fish market, the former Custom House (Fig 28), the Harbour Master's Office, warehouses and the current Royal Dorset Yacht Club, which was built in 1866 as a Sailor's Bethel.

The south side of the harbour in the 18th century was predominantly occupied by domestic buildings (Fig 29), the most famous being the house used by Ralph Allen (*see* Fig 6). Fashionable Georgian houses line Trinity Street and Trinity Road, while new, smaller houses were built in Cove Row around 1800; the inlet where Cove Row is now located was partially filled in during the late 18th century. Trinity Street also contains two houses of *c* 1600, indicating that even at an early date wealthy citizens lived in this area. Does the disparity between the buildings on the two sides of the harbour indicate that the original intention was for polite society to occupy the Weymouth side? Perhaps the numbers of visitors by the late 18th century led to a shift of emphasis in development on to the seafront of the Melcombe Regis side where there was room for growth.

As well as being a working quay and an attractive place to stay for fashionable people, the harbour was also the departure point for ferry services to the Channel Islands and France. In 1794 a packet service began to Guernsey and Jersey, and in 1827 a steam packet was introduced. In 1840 the Pile Pier (Fig 30) was created on the north side of the harbour, but with the opening of the railway from London to Southampton in the same year, Weymouth lost its advantage and the ferry service closed in April 1845. However, a new service opened in 1850 from Weymouth to St Malo, with stops in the Channel Islands, and with the opening of the railway to Weymouth in 1857 a new regular ferry service to the Channel Islands was inaugurated. The Pile Pier was rebuilt and extended in 1859–60 and in 1878 a new landing stage was completed. Further developments took place following an agreement in 1889 between the Great Western Railway and the Weymouth Corporation. The Corporation agreed to improve the harbour and build a new landing stage, baggage hall, offices and a refreshment room, while the railway company would introduce an improved steamer service. The other change in the late 19th century was at Hope Cove where some of the land reclaimed in the 1780s was removed, along with the houses on it. This was to make room for new, larger steamers to turn inside the harbour. In 1933 the Prince of Wales (the future Edward VIII) officially opened

Figure 29
Today visitors would not wish to stay near modern, industrial activity, but in the 18th century visitors were happy to be on the quayside, at the heart of the town. Many of the houses are now divided into flats or used as shops or restaurants.
[DP054481]

Figure 30
The Pile Pier, before its expansion during the later
19th century, was a fashionable promenade,
reminiscent of the Cobb at nearby Lyme Regis.
[Image courtesy of Charles Wagner; DP054544]

Figure 31
In contrast to the 'safe' bathing from the gently shelving
beach, sea bathing and particularly diving, was
conducted from the pier head and the headquarters of
the Weymouth Swimming Club was established here.
These bathing facilities were constructed in 1931–3.
[DP055559]

the new harbour and pier works. The existing pier was widened and a new extension added to accommodate the increased numbers of passenger and cargo vessels. The expansion also provided a public promenade, changing facilities and a diving stage for bathers (Fig 31).

Managing the growing resort

In the Middle Ages, Melcombe Regis and Weymouth were two settlements, each with their own local government, and despite their legal unification in 1571 they continued to have separate town halls. The unified Weymouth was one of the first seaside resorts to obtain an improvement act to allow a body of trustees to institute a series of improvements in the rapidly expanding town. The 1776 Improvement Act (16 Geo III c57) provided the trustees with an income from levying a rate and collecting tolls from turnpikes. This could be used as collateral to borrow £2,000 for major works, such as paving the roads, providing street lighting, creating pedestrian crossings and establishing new gutters, drains and wells. The improvement act also contained a special provision to eliminate thatched buildings. It stipulated that no new houses were to be covered with thatch and the thatch on any existing buildings had to be removed by 1 January 1784.

The principal focus of the act was on improving the roads, but at the beginning of the 19th century the largest infrastructure project was the construction of the sea wall. In the late 18th century, a turf-covered, earth bank protected the seafront buildings from the sea, but by 1800 this was deemed insufficient and work began on constructing a stone sea wall. This wall, built by two different contractors, ran from south to north and in 1805 Sir William Pulteney agreed to build a new sea wall running eastwards, parallel to the quay (Fig 32). In exchange for this, he was allowed to erect buildings on the land created by this embankment and this led to the construction of Pulteney Buildings and Devonshire Buildings (*see* Fig 21). In 1824 the sea wall was badly damaged by a severe storm, leading to major repairs. G A Ellis, writing only five years after the storm, vividly recorded the extent of the damage:

Figure 32
Since the early 19th century Weymouth has been protected by a solid sea wall. Sand now hides much of the walling, but some of the wall formed with large stone blocks is visible at the southern end of the Esplanade. In 1897, 63 sockets were fixed to the wall to hold flags. During the winter, fencing prevents sand from blowing up on to the Esplanade.
[DP024379]

[W]hole rows of houses that fronted the foaming, raging, billows, were completely inundated; the pride of Melcombe, its beautiful esplanade, was nearly all demolished, the stone posts and chains (which amount to 336 stone posts, and 4,620 feet of iron chain) were rent up and entirely broken, the piers … also were demolished, vessels, boats, and small craft, were either driven into the centre of the town, sunk, destroyed, or carried out to sea.[22]

A number of the posts and chains described by Ellis survive at the north end of the Esplanade, opposite the Pier Bandstand (Fig 33). And a marker called the Tempest Stone was made to commemorate the storm; it is now located in a flowerbed on the Esplanade and a replica has been placed in the rear wall of the tourist information centre.

The local council was also responsible for the bridge. The first bridge, built at the end of the 16th century, was replaced in 1713, 1741 and 1770 by other wooden bridges. The last of these was located approximately 70 metres to the west of the present site, at the foot of St Nicholas Street. In 1824 the first stone bridge opened on the traditional, and current, bridge site and this was substantially altered in 1880. This new bridge – called Town Bridge – had a

Figure 33
This historic photograph shows the Esplanade lined with small stone posts linked by chains.
[BB87/00005]

Figure 34
The Town Bridge is opened at regular intervals to allow yachts and power boats to move between the Marina in the Backwater and the historic part of the harbour, from where they can reach the sea. [DP054520]

central, cast-iron swing section. Its design is attributed to George Moneypenny, an architect who had specialised in prison design. The present Town Bridge was built in 1928–30 (Fig 34).

Victorian Weymouth

In the late 18th and early 19th centuries, Weymouth attracted affluent visitors primarily from the refined social scenes of London and Bath. Visitors could travel by coach from London to Dorchester, where they could catch another coach to Weymouth, and there was also a direct service from Bath. Slower and more uncomfortable transport in wagons was also available for servants and luggage.

As the 19th century progressed, the seaside became accessible to a wider section of society. The arrival of the railway in 1857 and the gradual introduction of paid holidays and bank holidays saw more visitors arriving in

Weymouth, including significant numbers on organised trips. An annual holiday from the Great Western Railway works in Swindon attracted thousands of visitors, and the 'Swindon Week', which latterly became the 'Swindon Fortnight', became a regular event at the beginning of July. At its peak almost 30,000 workers from the Great Western Railway works went by train to various destinations around England, with Weymouth – the most popular seaside destination – attracting over 6,000 of them in some years (Fig 35).

The advent of mass tourism placed the small-scale facilities of Georgian resorts under considerable strain and great efforts were made to provide both more open space to accommodate the holiday crowds and more extensive entertainment facilities. The seafront that greeted visitors to Weymouth in the second half of the 19th century was substantially the same as today, with all the major terraces being complete by the 1850s. However, the Esplanade was extended northwards from Brunswick Buildings in the 1880s and 1890s,

Figure 35
The annual Mechanics' Institute trip from Swindon was organised like a military operation. An instruction pamphlet told the workers where their allocated train could be boarded in the railway works and the time of departure.
[STEAM Museum of the Great Western Railway]

Figure 36
In 1889 the local authority decided to add a series
of shelters along the seafront. This photograph
was taken after the recent restoration programme,
part of a scheme to enhance the seafront.
[DP055545]

and in 1889 a set of shelters was added to the seafront (Fig 36). Originally, some of these had balconies projecting over the sands, much as the shelter at the south end, near the sand sculptures, does today; however, as the Esplanade is now wider, the shelters stand generally as isolated islands, set back from the sands.

The site of Alexandra Gardens was created from reclaimed land in the early 19th century, when it was used for grazing animals, but in 1867 it became public gardens. A bandstand was added in 1891 (Fig 37) and in 1904 six thatched shelters were built around the gardens. In 1913 the bandstand was enclosed with a glazed structure to create the Kursaal (Fig 38), but it was replaced in 1924 by the Alexandra Gardens Concert Hall. During the 1870s there was a fad for aquaria at seaside resorts and a scheme was discussed for an aquarium on the site of Alexandra Gardens, though this was never built. However, Weymouth did succumb to the new fashion of roller skating with rinks built in 1875 at the Burdon Hotel and in nearby Grange Road.

Figure 37
This postcard, of around 1905–10, shows
the bandstand before it was enclosed.
[PC07195]

Figure 38
A slightly later postcard shows the bandstand
after its enclosure to form the Kursaal.
[PC07196]

Figure 39
This photograph of c 1900 shows the beach with
bathing machines and the large bathing saloons.
Trailing behind the Ladies Saloon is a washing
line on which hired costumes are drying. One
bathing tent appears in the foreground.
[BB88/02329]

The initial driver for the expansion of seaside resorts had been a desire to improve health through sea bathing, but during the second half of the 19th century the emphasis changed. Bathing machines continued in use until the Second World War, but the strict etiquette associated with them was relaxed. Holidaymakers increasingly swam and bathed for pleasure as well as health, and to allow this, two sets of bathing saloons were introduced onto the seashore in 1890 (Fig 39). These resembled railway carriages and provided a number of changing rooms for bathers. Their inspiration appears to have been Walter David Fagg's 'New and Improved Safety Carriage', patented in 1888 and first used at Folkestone. These new facilities seem to have been blamed for a

new relaxed attitude to bathing and measures were taken to tighten this up. In 1897 the local council required that the male and female saloons should be 75 yards apart and this explains why, in some contemporary photos, the male and female saloons were separated by a line of bathing machines (Fig 40).

Changes to the seafront were relatively modest in the second half of the 19th century, but behind the seafront the town was growing rapidly. Much of this expansion on the Melcombe Regis side was on reclaimed land, continuing the process of reclamation that had transformed the shape of the town since the 16th century. The construction of the seafront terraces and the Esplanade consolidated some land on the seaward side of the town, and the site of Devonshire and Pulteney Buildings was reclaimed from the sea in the early 19th century. In February 1834 the decision was made to build a retaining wall

Figure 40
This 1930s postcard, advertising the restaurant in the Clinton Arcade, shows how the remaining bathing machines were used to enforce the separation between the male and female saloons.
[DP024380]

to reclaim 50 acres along the Backwater (the wide part of the River Wey to the east of Weymouth) and the railway station was built on this land in the 1850s. During the late 19th century, substantial developments took place on new land in the area around the station. Most of this was domestic in character, but these were also the homes where new arrivals could find inexpensive rooms to lodge in (Fig 41). During the Swindon Week, hordes of Swindonians would arrive with their week's food ready for their landladies to cook or heat up. In contrast, during the late 19th century, wealthier visitors could still avail themselves of the comforts of the Georgian Royal Hotel and, from the late 1850s, the new Burdon Hotel (Figs 42 and 43).

Figure 42
The original Royal Hotel was demolished in 1891. The exuberant exterior of its successor is strikingly different from the more austere Georgian terraces that line the seafront. [AA037560]

Figure 43
The Burdon Hotel, now known as the Prince Regent Hotel, was the grand
centrepiece of Victoria Terrace. It was differentiated from flanking terrace
houses because of its size and by the use of canted bays rather than balconies.
[DP055527]

On the south side of the harbour the pace of development was slower, and was on existing, rather than reclaimed, land. However, the most substantial developments in the late 19th century took place on the west side of the Backwater. In the 1860s the only building on the west bank of the river was the gas works, but by 1900 houses had been built in the area between the railway line to Portland and the Backwater, and a major development had taken place along Abbotsbury Road and in flanking streets.

The changing character and taste of visitors had an impact on the entertainment facilities in seaside resorts. Assembly rooms, theatres and libraries continued through the 19th century, but these relatively exclusive institutions were gradually replaced by entertainment facilities that could accommodate the growing masses arriving at resorts. For instance, the Theatre Royal closed in 1859 and a new Theatre Royal opened in a former Congregational chapel in 1865. In guidebooks this is variously described as a theatre or a music hall, but it was still relatively small scale. Its closure in 1893 was probably a result of competition from the Jubilee Hall, which was built in 1887 and designed by Crickmay and Sons with an auditorium capable of holding between 2,000 and 3,000 people (Fig 44). Although originally built as a hall, it was converted into a theatre in the 1890s and later became a cinema, then a bingo hall until its closure and demolition in 1989 (Fig 45).

Weymouth in the 20th century

Although the railways had introduced new visitors to the charms of Weymouth and fashions might have changed, late Victorian visitors were still pursuing a holiday that would have been recognisable to their Georgian forebears. During the 20th century, new technologies, longer paid holidays, increased affluence and cheaper foreign holidays transformed the nature of the seaside holiday in England, yet Weymouth seems to have been able to balance these new demands with preserving the best of its past.

Weymouth was still promoted as a genteel health resort immediately after the First World War. Although it did not have a winter season comparable to Bournemouth and Brighton, attempts were made to attract visitors outside

Figure 44
During the demolition of Jubilee Hall the elaborate
structure of the original building was uncovered.
This main space was 118ft long and 60ft wide
(36m by 18m) with side aisles and its roof was
carried on arched, laminated wood trusses.
[DP024387]

Figure 45
Jubilee Hall was demolished in 1989 and by
2000 its site had been occupied by the New
Bond Street retail development (see Fig 62).
[DP024388]

the summer season; guidebooks described autumn as 'sunny and bracing' and the winter months before Christmas were reported as 'delightful'.[23] The Municipal Orchestra, which played at Alexandra Gardens, started its performances in May, and the orchestra at the Pavilion tea room played throughout the year.

Health remained a key theme in Weymouth's advertising even into the 1970s, when guidebooks encouraged visitors and businesses to relocate for the climate and environment. The beach remained home to bathing machines and bathing saloons until the Second World War and, in 1934, the Weymouth Bathing Saloon Company ran 6 large saloons and 32 family machines on the beach (see Fig 39). The saloons could accommodate 56 bathers in individual cabins and the family machines each had space for 4 people. During the 1920s bathing tents, manufactured locally by Messrs Marsh & Wright, dotted the beach and these could be hired from offices in the Royal Arcade. Gentlemen could bathe separately from the beach beside Greenhill Gardens and, due to the steeper slope of the beach, diving rafts were provided offshore. The popularity of bathing in this area is demonstrated by the construction in 1923 of one- and two-storied chalets, known as the Beach Bungalows or Beach Chalets (Fig 46). Changing facilities and diving rafts were also provided at the end of the pier and this was the most popular venue for those wishing to dive into deeper water.

While Weymouth's more informal facilities were being improved, the closure of the Royal Baths in 1927 ended a 150-year tradition of indoor seawater bathing. It was not until 1974 that a new swimming complex was opened, though as this was located in Westham, rather than the town centre, it was clearly a facility for residents rather than visitors.

An official guide to Weymouth, published in 1925, described the resort as being 'an intensely modern seaside town',[24] but to maintain its currency with existing visitors, as well as attracting new ones, there was a need for some new buildings, within and around the town. The two major additions to the seafront in the 20th century were the Pavilion Theatre and the Pier Bandstand. The Pavilion (Fig 47), as it was first known, was situated at the southern end of the Esplanade on reclaimed land beside the Pile Pier. Built in 1908, it had an auditorium that could seat 1,200. It was destroyed by fire in 1954 and the present Pavilion Theatre opened in 1960 (Fig 48). The Pier Bandstand opened

Figure 46
Built at a cost of £11,000, the Beach Chalets were constructed as part of a local authority employment scheme. They consisted of 45 rooms in a two-storied block and a single-storied section of 16 rooms. The flat roofs were used as promenades and sun decks.
[DP055514]

Figure 47
Built by the local authority, the Pavilion was much more than a theatre; at various times it housed a tea room, dining rooms, private rooms and refreshment buffets. The first-floor terraces were used for promenading and at the east side there was a roller-skating rink that was transformed into the Royal Palm Court ballroom. The site also included hard tennis courts.
[DP024382]

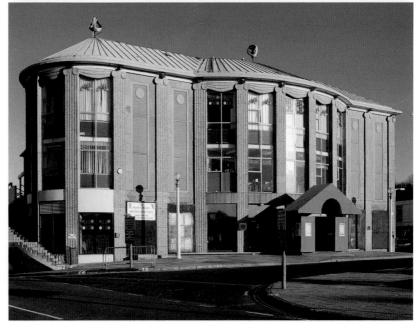

Figure 48
The Pavilion Theatre was designed by the Verity & Beverley partnership, which had designed a number of cinemas for Paramount in the 1930s. Due to weather damage, the decorative shell and pebble panels that adorned the front elevation between the fluted Ionic 'pilasters' were covered in the 1980s. There are plans for the theatre to be remodelled under the proposed Weymouth Pavilion Theatre and Ferry Terminal Site scheme.
[DP055606]

in 1939 on the seafront opposite Victoria Terrace (Fig 49). It consisted of a two-storied block on the promenade with a deck extending out to sea between the high- and low-water marks. This deck, which had a seating capacity of 2,400, was open in the centre with glazed shelters around the sides leading to the bandstand at the seaward end. It was demolished in 1986, leaving the entrance block, which had been redesigned in the 1960s, to house an amusement arcade and restaurant.

With the increase in car and caravan ownership during the mid- and late 20th century, large developments began to take place beyond the traditional boundaries of the town. This was most evident at Bowleaze Cove, where L Stewart Smith's modernist, Spanish-style Riviera Hotel was built in 1937 (Figs 50 and 51). Waterside Caravan Camp was established to the north and west of the hotel in the 1950s, transforming the formerly deserted cove into a lively holiday centre, and two further holiday parks were later laid out between Bowleaze Cove and Preston (Fig 52). At Osmington, the Shortlake House estate was developed into a holiday centre in the 1930s and this became Fred Pontin's second holiday camp in 1946 (Fig 53). This adult-only camp, described in 1972 as 'the place to whoop it up' and 'the swing camp of the south',[25] was sold off in 1999 and is now, ironically, a children's adventure holiday centre.

To the south of Weymouth, Chesil Beach Holiday Park opened on the site of the former Port Sanitary Authority Hospital, incorporating two wards into modernised guest accommodation. At Chickerell, Littlesea Camp (now Littlesea Holiday Park) was established after the Second World War, offering a self-contained site for tents and caravans. These new sites led to a fundamental shift in the pattern of holiday accommodation, so that by 1984, 48.3 per cent of all tourist bed spaces in Weymouth were provided by static caravans, touring caravans and tents. In 1936 an architectural writer described Butlins' first holiday camp at Ingoldmells in Lincolnshire as 'a remarkable venture', but he warned against the spread of Elizabethan-style chalets to Dorset's cliffs.[26] The timber-framed chalets were avoided, but the march of the caravan could not be resisted.

Figure 53
Built on the cliff top to the south of the village of Osmington, this Pontin's site has been host to holidaymakers for nearly 80 years. It comprises terraces of holiday chalets, communal facilities and areas for outdoor activities, and has access to the fine sandy beach below.
[NMR 21662/12]

One theme in Weymouth's development, both before and after the Second World War, has been the desire to provide public spaces, for residents as well as visitors. Reclamation in the 19th century had created the Alexandra Gardens and in the 1920s Melcombe Regis Gardens were created on land reclaimed from Radipole Lake. Much of the site is now a car park, although the bowling green and some of the glasshouses survive. A further survivor is the former Noah's Ark Aquarium, built at the edge of the gardens in 1966 (Fig 54).

Weymouth also had gardens beside the Nothe Fort and at Greenhill (Fig 55), where in 1923 a local authority employment scheme included new landscaping, the re-laying of tennis courts, an extension of the bowling green and the construction of the chalet complex on the Esplanade (*see* Fig 46). The newest, public open space is Lodmoor Country Park. In 1958 the council proposed using it for car parking, a boating lake, an amusement park, playing fields, a helicopter station and a holiday camp; however, Butlins and other companies did not want to develop the site. One of the aims for developing the country park was to provide alternative attractions away from the beach, some of which would not be dependent on good weather. Facilities now include a nature reserve, the Weymouth Sea Life Adventure Park and Marine Sanctuary, a miniature railway, a pitch-and-putt golf course and an outdoor events area.

Figure 54
Melcombe Regis Gardens included tennis courts, a bowling green, putting greens, a rose walk, an 'Arnold Palmer gadget golf course' and the glasshouses belonging to the Corporation Nursery. The former Noah's Ark Aquarium was constructed on a hull-shaped concrete base, but by the mid-1970s the site had become an amusement arcade and later a restaurant.
[DP055567]

Figure 55
Greenhill Gardens has been a popular retreat at the north end of the Esplanade for over a century and it originally marked the northernmost extent of development on the seafront. It now lies between mid-19th-century and early 20th-century housing schemes on the seafront.
[PC08972]

Funding for the leisure developments at Lodmoor was provided by selling some of the land at the periphery for housing.

During the August bank holiday in 1939, around 100,000 visitors flocked to Weymouth, but a few days later Britain was at war. Weymouth was declared a defence area, meaning that visiting the resort became difficult and the beach was cleared of its bathing machines and closed. Hordes of civilian visitors were replaced by regiments of billeted troops and many of the resort's attractions were taken over by the military or closed. The theatre in Alexandra Gardens was requisitioned, the Pavilion Theatre was closed for the duration of the war, Nothe Gardens was declared out of bounds to civilians and the Royal Hotel became the local headquarters of the United States military. Security was further tightened prior to D-Day, as much of the US assault force was launched from the harbours at Weymouth and Portland. Between D-Day and VE-Day, 517,816 troops and 144,093 vehicles set sail from the harbours. Several monuments commemorate Weymouth's wartime history (Fig 56).

Due to the town's military significance, it was subject to scores of air raids, leading to over 1,200 houses being destroyed or severely damaged. Weymouth's High Street was badly damaged and largely demolished after the war and the nearby Chapelhay area was rebuilt in the 1950s, with the flats and shops of Chapelhay Heights replacing the bombed, terraced streets. However, Weymouth's resort infrastructure survived relatively untouched and in the summer of 1945 visitors were already able to return in significant numbers to enjoy the newly reopened beach.

The immediate post-war period was difficult for England's seaside resorts. They were not seen as a priority for local or national government investment and until the late 20th century no major architectural projects of distinction were undertaken at the seaside. Instead local authorities usually revived existing pre-war facilities and invested modestly on maintaining their seafronts (Fig 57). By the 1970s increased affluence allowed Britons the unprecedented option of an affordable holiday on hot Mediterranean beaches. The lure of the novel and exotic that once brought people to England's seaside was now taking them abroad. Although England's seaside was still regarded with affection, it could not compete with new, purpose-built facilities and warmer climates, and soon the charming nostalgic image was superseded by newspaper headlines proclaiming the terminal decline of the seaside.

Figure 56
Seaside promenades have always been a popular venue for major works of public sculpture and memorials, performing the role of a marketplace or public park in other towns. The Esplanade includes Weymouth's First World War and Second World War Memorial (seen here), the American Memorial and the ANZAC Memorial.
[DP055529]

Figure 57
Sluice Gardens, at the northern end of the Esplanade, was formed on the northern side of the sluice that drained water from Lodmoor to the sea. They were redesigned in 1961 to contain 23 chalets in 3 terraces, a children's paddling pool and a sandpit.
[DP055505]

Some resorts have responded to the new challenges by opting for significant new development and a major scheme that would have destroyed much of Weymouth's historic centre was mooted in the 1960s. Fortunately, this scheme was never undertaken and now the presumption at Weymouth and other seaside resorts is that the historic environment will be a key element in the future success of seaside towns.

CHAPTER 3

Weymouth in the 21st century

During the late 20th century, Weymouth, like other seaside resorts, succumbed to the widespread dash to the sun. Facing strong competition from foreign resorts, the town's provision of leisure and entertainment facilities failed to match the increasing, and changing, demands of visitors. At the same time the town centre's role as a shopping centre also began to fail to meet the demands of retailers and their customers.

This process of gradual decline was accompanied from the 1960s by an increasing trend in town planning towards the dominance of the motor vehicle, with proposals for Weymouth which, though not all implemented, had the result of favouring traffic over the pedestrian in key areas of the town. A struggling retail market during the 1980s had an effect on the local economy and the downturn was exacerbated in the 1990s by a round of defence cuts. The closure of Portland Naval Base and the adjoining Fleet Air Arm Station, and the relocation of most of the associated MOD research establishments and many of the companies that supplied products for the navy led to the loss of 4,500 local jobs, many of them of a specialist nature and, consequently, well paid. In a borough with a population of just over 60,000, this was a major setback, particularly in the way that it undermined the year-round economy.

This combination of changing holiday patterns and economic decline had a significant impact on the fabric of Weymouth. The increasing demand for self-catering accommodation, usually in caravans or chalets on self-contained sites on the outskirts of the town or elsewhere in south Dorset, provided a significant threat to traditional holiday accommodation within the historic town. The reduction in demand for serviced accommodation in smaller hotels and guest houses discouraged investment in the upkeep of the fabric of many seafront buildings and the businesses they housed. In addition declining visitor numbers reduced the funds available for maintenance and improvement, a problem that became more acute with the increasing demand for en suite facilities.

Dependence on a seasonal trade and the decrease in visitor numbers led some owners to convert their buildings to other uses. Some houses have been converted into 'Houses in Multiple Occupation' (HMO), often inhabited by a transient population with limited financial resources (Fig 58). This function relied less on the appearance of buildings for their operation, leading to a

The Georgian houses on the harbour side now co-exist with modern fishing and pleasure boats. [AA037566]

further, and marked, visual deterioration in parts of the town. Fortunately, this phenomenon has not had a major impact on Weymouth's most precious built asset, its seafront.

In addition to a gradual deterioration in the condition of some of its buildings, by the 1990s parts of the public realm of Weymouth – despite attempts at constant maintenance – were suffering both physically and visually, particularly along the seafront. This was partly due to the harsh coastal environment, but an increasing amount of poor signage and associated street clutter has contributed to the sense of decline, undermining the day-to-day experiences of residents and visitors alike. When coupled with an ongoing concern for the built fabric of the town, problems with traffic congestion and a recognition that the underpinning economy needed a comprehensive boost, it was clear that a dramatic and effective intervention was necessary to guarantee the future of Weymouth.

The past 40 years have seen a number of significant initiatives designed to inject a new vibrancy into Weymouth's economy and environment. Belief in the 1960s that historic buildings should not stand in the way of creating successful town centres was superseded by a growing realisation that the town's future success was inextricably linked to the preservation of its distinctive historic qualities. The major schemes that have affected the town in this period demonstrate efforts to balance economic development with retention of character. The balance shifts within each scheme and there has been loss of historic fabric, but conservation is about promoting the historic environment within the context of changing needs and values, not simply about preservation. Weymouth's recent history illustrates perfectly the way in which numerous interests are brought to bear in the search for economic health and a vibrant, purposeful historic environment.

Weymouth's historic character is recognised formally in the systems of designations that seek to identify and protect its buildings and areas of special significance. The value of the town's heritage is reflected in the number of its historic buildings that are listed and in the designation in 1974 of the Town Centre Conservation Area. During the subsequent 25 years the size of the conservation area was increased to include the southern side of the harbour, the Backwater, the Swannery, the streets behind the Esplanade and, at the end of the 20th century, Greenhill.

Figure 58
In Crescent Street, immediately behind the seafront, there are many Georgian and Victorian buildings that have not been well maintained. Houses once occupied by families, and during the summer by lodgers, have now been divided into inexpensive flats. [DP024384]

Schemes to reuse and enhance areas of historic fabric in the town have already proven their economic and social benefit. When the Devenish Brewery in Hope Square closed in 1985, the future potential of its collection of historic brewing buildings was recognised and the buildings were retained and reused as the basis for new enterprises (Fig 59). These substantial industrial buildings, typical of the historic industrial structures that were once swept away in the

Figure 59
Brewers Quay, an area that was once dominated by derelict brewing buildings, is now a 'destination' for visitors and residents, and the square is used for events and entertainment.
[DP054467]

name of progress, were converted into a vibrant complex containing leisure, entertainment, residential and retail uses. Their conversion has created a new space within the town and its positive impact has allowed existing pubs, cafés and shops to become busy outlets that, alongside new business enterprises, are reviving the area (Fig 60).

Changing attitudes to the historic environment are evident in Weymouth in the absence of the sort of large-scale redevelopment that has dramatically altered the character and appearance of many other historic urban areas in the country. While such activity might have been welcomed in the not too distant past as a means of enhancing the town's retail profile, its absence has had the beneficial effect of allowing the essential qualities of Weymouth to survive largely unravaged by late 20th-century development trends. Proposals for major road improvements, which originated in the 1960s and could have had serious implications for the historic fabric of the town, were shelved. In their place more modest proposals for one-way traffic and semi-pedestrianisation schemes have been introduced (Fig 61).

However, there has been some development in the town over the past 20 years. Concern over the trading fortunes of the town centre saw the emergence in 1985 of the *Weymouth Town Centre Consultative Document*. This led to the building of a retail development, which was completed in 2000 and included a multiplex cinema and a department store (Fig 62). Although this scheme retained much of the historic street pattern and enabled four listed buildings to be restored and incorporated into the development, it led to the

Figure 63
Many long-term residents, as well as visitors, cannot understand why the council has allowed the gasworks and other public utility and municipal buildings on the west side of the Backwater to occupy this prime location. The fact that most of these date back to the late 19th and early 20th centuries is now forgotten.
[NMR 21660/004]

loss of some significant historic fabric and the creation of a large, dominant building. While it is tempting to consider whether such a scheme would be considered acceptable now, it is important to bear in mind the hopes that it embodied and the strength of the commercial and political imperatives that existed at the time.

Contemporary with the town centre development, and driven by similar economic considerations, the Backwater was transformed into the Inner Harbour and Marina, and residential development started to replace a series of modest commercial and industrial buildings lining the east bank (Fig 63). In this way the 'back' of the town facing the Backwater became a new frontage facing the Inner Harbour, with a contemporary character that began to replace that of its industrial and commercial past (Fig 64).

Figure 64
Beside Town Bridge, on the north side of the river, there is an example of new development alongside substantial old warehouses that have now been converted into apartments.
[DP055594]

Weymouth acknowledged that new facilities and attractions were essential for the creation of a prosperous town, but it also recognised the role that the town's historic fabric played in defining its character and in supporting the continued existence of many of its traditional businesses. This led to the creation of a Town Scheme in 1984, which ran until 1997. Through a series of grants, funded by a partnership between English Heritage, Dorset County Council and Weymouth & Portland Borough Council, the scheme was responsible for the repair of historic buildings in the town centre. As well as improving the appearance of individual buildings, the scheme also contributed to an improvement in the overall appearance of streets.

The life of the Town Scheme coincided with the decision by the borough council to invest in its own estate of historic buildings along the Esplanade, most of them hotels and all listed. This programme, involving over £1.3m of local authority funds supplemented by English Heritage grants, helped to highlight the ongoing problems affecting hotels in the town. The council's freehold ownership of most of the hotels and guest houses on the Esplanade, combined with planning policies, has meant that the problems associated with HMOs have been kept away from the seafront. However, a review of the length and nature of the council's often short leases recognised the need to provide the hotels with greater certainty of tenure and, therefore, a more robust basis for future investment. Some were also sold off in an effort to stimulate private investment in the hotel sector (Fig 65).

The Town Scheme was followed by a Conservation Area Partnership (CAP) between 1995 and 1998. This involved the same funding partners and was focussed on the Esplanade. By the time that the CAP scheme had concluded, the benefit of investment in the town's historic fabric was beginning to be recognised. New planning policies were introduced to provide more effective protection for the historic character of the town, and attention had been drawn to the need for an integrated approach to the enhancement of the Esplanade.

While such multi-million pound aspirations might have existed, it was difficult to identify how they could be realised, but finding a solution was assisted by developments on Portland. Following the departure of the MOD from the island, the South West of England Regional Development Agency (SWRDA) acquired the site to secure its future regeneration and a strategic master plan was created for the area now known as Osprey Quay. Over the past

Figure 65
The seafront terraced houses are now mostly occupied by small hotels and guest houses. In the distance is the Royal Hotel (see Figs 17 and 42). [DP024385]

decade a range of recreational activities and businesses have been established, capitalising on its location and the existing maritime infrastructure. The new Weymouth & Portland National Sailing Academy was established in 1999 and in 2005 a purpose-built clubhouse and training centre opened. Together with the excellent local sailing conditions, the existence of this facility was key to the selection of Portland as the site for the London 2012 Olympic and Paralympic Games sailing events and this decision has prompted a reconsideration of the infrastructure and facilities of the wider area upon which a successful event would depend.

This international spotlight has also generated valuable political and commercial interest in Weymouth. A Townscape Heritage Initiative (THI), which began in 2006, has established a fund of £1.13m, including money from the Heritage Lottery Fund. Targeting the repair and restoration of historic buildings and structures along the seafront and in streets in the immediately adjacent area, the THI also led to the commissioning of an Urban Landscape Appraisal and Masterplan that focussed on the Esplanade. The Masterplan contained proposals for improving the appearance of the public realm along the Esplanade and recommended ways to reduce the conflict between vehicles and pedestrians. It also included strategies for the townscape, street lighting and street furniture (Fig 66). These proposals, and the recommendations that emerged from a Conservation Area Character Appraisal, were embodied in a management plan for the area. Detailed proposals were worked up into a design guide for the seafront and form the basis of a bid for funding from the SWRDA (Figs 67 and 68). Collectively, these schemes seek to enhance the appeal of the town, harnessing the character of Weymouth's historic buildings and integrating new, improved infrastructure and amenities.

While these initiatives aim to address the physical and management issues affecting the Esplanade as a whole, land at its southern end has long been identified as an area for redevelopment. This site houses the Pavilion Theatre and Ferry Terminal and a large area of surface car parking (Fig 69). Owned by the borough council, a scheme now exists for the creation of a modernised Pavilion Theatre, a Jurassic Coast World Heritage Centre, a four-star hotel, a new public square, cafés, retail outlets, residential units, associated parking and a marina. The council has established a partnership with a development company and more detailed designs for the site are being drawn up.

Figure 66
Some of the shelters on the seafront have already been restored, but the Victorian lighting columns are still cluttered with haphazard arrangements of lights, loudspeakers and signs that have accrued over recent years.
[DP024386]

Collectively, it is intended that the development of the Pavilion Theatre site, the enhancement of the Esplanade and the repair of its historic buildings, and the building of a new relief road will be completed by 2012. Not only should these projects ensure that the area plays its part in the delivery of a successful Olympic and Paralympic Games, but they will also provide a sustainable legacy for the whole community upon which the future of Weymouth can hopefully be assured.

Weymouth is fortunate to have a particularly rich seaside heritage, stretching back to the origin of this peculiarly British phenomenon. It is clear that alongside the new challenges and opportunities that now face the resort, the historic town, its bustling harbour and the long, elegant seafront will all play a vital part in its future.

Seaside resorts are the creation of over 250 years of holidaymaking – from Georgian bathers, through the time of the heavily dressed Victorian holidaymaker, to the 20th-century day tripper. All have left their mark on

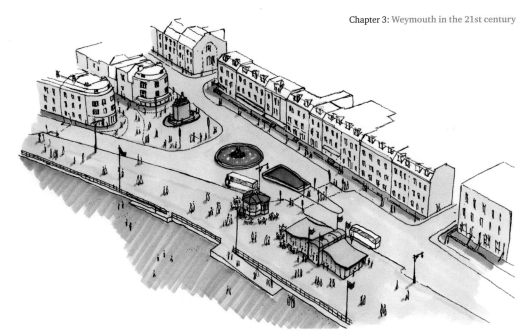

Figure 67
The SWRDA bid is for a
comprehensive package of inter-
related schemes, These include
the provision of public-realm
'gateways' – focal points on the
Esplanade and promenade,
including a new 'square'
around George III's statue.
[Watkins Dally Landscape
Architects]

Figure 68
The Pier Bandstand was a bold new venture
immediately before the Second World War,
but it has suffered from major demolitions
and new additions in the post-war years. In
the future it should become a focal point for
activities at the north end of the Esplanade.
[Watkins Dally Landscape Architects]

Figure 69
The Pavilion Theatre and Ferry Terminal
stand on a large area of land reclaimed from
the sea. This arrangement is the successor to
the jetty and piers mentioned on p 30.
[NMR 21661/09]

seaside towns, and seaside towns have left their mark on us, featuring prominently in everyone's memories. Promoting what makes seaside towns special should help make tourists' visits more enjoyable, but it will also help to engender a strong sense of pride in the place for residents.

Successful conservation regeneration depends upon understanding and appreciating historic places and recognition of the significance of elements within them. That understanding should shape the thinking behind redevelopment and reflect the values placed on the historic environment, not just by 'experts' or developers, but by the whole community. An appreciation of Weymouth's distinctive past can be a positive force for its future.

Notes

Bibliographical Note: The publishers of Georgian guidebooks often omitted publication dates to avoid their books being considered out-of-date by visitors to resorts. Here the dates given (followed by ?) are estimated dates of publication.

1 Theroux, P 1983 *The Kingdom by the Sea*. London: Penguin, 98

2 Toulmin Smith, L (ed) 1964 *The Itinerary of John Leland in or About the Years 1535–1543, Vol 1*. London: Centaur Press, 304

3 Coker, J 1980 *Coker's Survey of Dorsetshire*. Sherborne: Dorset Publishing, 34

4 Defoe, D 1968 *A Tour thro' the Whole Island of Great Britain, Vol 1*. London: Frank Cass & Co Ltd, 212

5 Moule 1883, 125

6 Berg, T and P (transl), 2001 *R R Angerstein's Illustrated Travel Diary 1753–1755*. London: Science Museum, 69

7 Burney, F 1941 *The Diary of Fanny Burney*. London: Dent, 254

8 Anon 1977 *The Marine Residence and Household Furniture of His Late Majesty at Weymouth in the County of Dorset: The particulars and conditions of sale of … Gloucester Lodge*. St Peter Port: Toucan Press

9 Anon 1797?, *A New Weymouth Guide*. Dorchester, 16

10 Bruyn Andrews, C (ed) 1934 *The Torrington Diaries 1781–1794*. London: Eyre and Spottiswoode, 87

11 Commins, J 1836 *Commins's Improved Weymouth Guide*. Weymouth: J Commins, 32

12 Commins 1836, 78

13 Bruyn Andrews 1934, 87

14 Anon 1785?, *The Weymouth Guide …*. Weymouth, 57

15 Anon 1797?, 15

16 Anon 1797?, 21

17 Commins 1836, 28–9

18 Burney 1941, 257

19 Carey, G S 1799 *The Balnea*. London: West & Hughes, 113

20 Henstock, A (ed) 1980 *The Diary of Abigail Gawthern of Nottingham 1751–1810*, Thoroton Society Record Series. Nottingham: Thoroton Society of Nottingham, 33

21 Bruyn Andrews 1934, 93

22 Ellis, G A 1829 *The History and Antiquities of the Borough and Town of Weymouth and Melcombe Regis*. Weymouth, 131–2

23 House, E E (ed) 1925 *Weymouth The Official Publication of the Corporation*. The Health Resorts Association, 13; Anon 1919 *The 'Borough' Guide To Weymouth*. Cheltenham: E J Burrow & Co, 14

24 House 1925, 13

25 Anon 1972 *Pontin's Holidays* (summer brochure), 15

26 Brenan, H B 1936 'The Visitor', *The Architectural Review*, **LXXX**, July, 15

Further reading

Attwooll, M and Pomeroy, C A 2004 *Weymouth Century*. Tiverton: Dorset Books

Attwooll, M 2006 *The Bumper Book of Weymouth*. Tiverton: Halsgrove

Boddy, M and West, J 1995 *Weymouth: An illustrated history*. Wimborne: The Dovecote Press

Brodie, A, Sargent, A and Winter, G 2005 *Seaside Holidays in the Past*. London: English Heritage

Brodie, A and Winter, G 2007 *England's Seaside Resorts*. London: English Heritage

Fletcher, G 1986 *Draft Weymouth Area Local Plan*. Weymouth Borough Council

Herbert, G and Attwooll, M 2003 *Weymouth: The golden years*. Tiverton: Dorset Books

Herbert, G and Attwooll, M 2003 *Weymouth: More golden years. A companion volume to Weymouth: The golden years*. Tiverton: Dorset Books

Hutchins, J 1774 *The History and Antiquities of the County of Dorset*. London: W Bowyer and J Nichols

Moule, H J 1883 *Descriptive Catalogue of the Charters, Minute Books, and Other Documents, of the Borough of Weymouth and Melcombe Regis. AD 1252 to 1800. With extracts and some notes*. Weymouth: Sherren & Son

RCHME 1970 *An Inventory of Historical Monuments in the County Of Dorset, Vol Two: South-East, Part 2*. London: HMSO

Ricketts, E 1975–6 *The Buildings of Old Weymouth, Parts 1 and 2*. Weymouth: Longman's of Weymouth

Gazetteer of Weymouth's principal buildings of interest

Nothe Fort, Barrack Road. [DP055586]

(1) Nothe Fort, Barrack Road

The Nothe Fort was mainly built between *c* 1860 and 1872 by troops from the Royal Engineers. The fort remained in active service until 1956. In 1979 Weymouth Civic Society obtained a licence to restore the site, transforming it into a museum.

(2) Former Red Barracks/Wellington Court, Barrack Road (*see* Fig 7)

The former barracks – known as Red Barracks due to the colour of the brickwork – were completed in the mid-1790s, but they were rebuilt at the start of the 19th century following a fire in 1798. After the Second World War, the buildings were little used and during the 1980s they were converted into flats.

(3) Brewers Quay, Hope Square (*see* Fig 59)

The complex of brewery buildings facing Hope Square includes Arthur Kinder's 1903–4 range, which was built for Groves' Brewery and later incorporated into Devenish Brewery in 1960. Following closure, the site was developed into a mixed cultural and retail centre, opening as Brewers Quay in 1990.

Brewers Quay, Hope Square. [DP054469]

(4) Old Rooms Inn, 16–17 Trinity Street and Cove Row (*see* Figs 16 and 26)

A two-storied brick building was added to the rear of a late 16th-century house to serve as the resort's first assembly room. It had ceased to be used for this function by 1785 due to the success of the assembly room in the Royal Hotel in Gloucester Row on the Esplanade.

(5) Ralph Allen's House, 2–2A Trinity Road (*see* Fig 6)

Dating from the second half of the 18th century, and later raised and extended, 2–2A Trinity Road was the site of the house reputedly occupied by Ralph Allen between 1750 and 1764. It was refurbished in 2008.

Town Bridge. [DP055595]

(6) Town Bridge (*see* Fig 34)

The Town Bridge was officially opened on 4 July 1930 by the Duke of York (later George VI). It was on the traditional site of several bridges since the 16th century, though from 1770 to 1824 Weymouth's bridge was located 70 metres to the west.

(9) Pavilion Theatre, The Esplanade
(*see* Figs 48 and 69)

The original Pavilion was built on reclaimed land beside the Pile Pier in 1908, but a fire destroyed the building in 1954. In 1960 a new Pavilion Theatre, designed by the Verity & Beverley partnership, opened on the original site.

Site of bathhouse (on far left of image), Custom House Quay. [AA036119]

Pavilion Theatre, The Esplanade. [DP055602]

(7) Former warehouse/Deep Sea Adventure, 9 Custom House Quay
(*see* Fig 28)

This 19th-century warehouse is an example of a successful conversion of a historic industrial building into a tourist attraction. Hanney's Fish Warehouse, later John Deheer's Warehouse, was mainly used for storing imported fertilisers. After closing in 1965, the building has subsequently been converted into a children's play centre and maritime exhibition attraction.

(8) Site of bathhouse, Custom House Quay

Hot and cold seawater baths were available at a late 18th-century bathhouse on the quayside of Melcombe Regis. The bathhouse was located on the site of the present Royal Dorset Yacht Club headquarters, the former Sailor's Bethel; at one time the yacht club headquarters were located in the former library (*see* pp 24 and 73).

(10) Pier Bathing Station, Pleasure Pier (*see* Fig 31)

In the 1920s the Corporation added facilities for swimmers, including changing cubicles and diving rafts. Following the extension of the pier in 1931–3, new bathing facilities were constructed and the remains of this bathing station form the base of the present Cactus Tea Rooms.

(11) Devonshire Buildings, 1–6 The Esplanade (*see* Fig 21)

Built on reclaimed land at the beginning of the 19th century, Devonshire Buildings is the Esplanade's southernmost seafront terrace. No. 1, The Roundhouse, replaced an original, rectangular house that terminated the terrace. Built in *c* 1819, its curved shape echoes the forms of Statue House and 1 Coburg Place, opposite the statue of George III.

Devonshire Buildings, 1–6 The Esplanade. [DP054505]

Alexandra Gardens, The Esplanade. [PC08974]

(12) Pulteney Buildings, 7–15 The Esplanade

Nos 7–12 were probably built shortly before the adjacent Devonshire Buildings, and were named after Sir William Pulteney who had taken the opportunity to reclaim land at the southern end of the Esplanade. The remaining three houses, at the west end, were built in the mid-19th century.

(13) Former sanatorium, Clarence Buildings, 19 The Esplanade (*see* Fig 15)

Weymouth Sanatorium was founded in 1848 for the reception of women and children. A purpose-built building, erected in 1862–3 to provide additional accommodation, was designed by the local architect G R Crickmay. Being close to the busy harbour was not ideal and therefore the sanatorium moved to a new site at Greenhill in 1902.

(14) Alexandra Gardens, The Esplanade (*see* Figs 37 and 38)

Land at the southern end of the Esplanade was acquired by George Stephenson in 1867 and was donated to the town to provide the resort's first public gardens. This was the site of a bandstand, then the Kursaal, which was replaced in 1924 by the Alexandra Gardens Concert Hall. It closed in 1963 and was converted into an amusement arcade, which was destroyed by fire in 1993.

(15) Site of Theatre Royal, 44 The Esplanade

Weymouth's first theatre, which opened in 1771, was situated on the seafront at 10 Augusta Place, just to the south of Bond Street. Its last performance was in 1859. The site of the theatre is now occupied by Banus Nightclub.

(16) Former library, 51 The Esplanade (*see* Figs 19 and 25)

Dating from the early 1780s and originally called Harvey's Library, this was the first purpose-built library in the resort and was originally freestanding. The building later became the first headquarters of the Royal Dorset Yacht Club.

(17) Charlotte Row, 47–50 The Esplanade, and York Buildings, 52–7 The Esplanade (*see* Fig 19)

The first of the seafront, terraced-house developments, York Buildings was built in *c* 1783–5 as a terrace of seven, three-storied houses with basements and attics. Charlotte Row, on the other side of the circulating library, was added a decade later.

(18) Site of Jubilee Hall and Arcadia (*see* Figs 44 and 45)

Built in 1887, Jubilee Hall was Weymouth's largest entertainment venue. Designed by local architects Crickmay and Sons, it was converted into a theatre in the 1890s, and in 1926 it became a cinema. Arcadia was on the north side of Jubilee Hall. Initially an open-air venue for roller skating, it was covered in 1911 to provide a dance hall. The site was cleared in 1989 to make way for Debenhams and the New Bond Street development.

(19) Frederick Place, 1–12 St Thomas Street

Completed in *c* 1834, Frederick Place is a terrace of 12 houses extending north from the Masonic Hall, which was built in 1816 and refronted around the same time that the terrace was built. Frederick Terrace was built on part of the Shrubbery, the gardens of Gloucester Lodge.

(20) Site of Royal Baths, St Thomas Street and St Mary Street (*see* Fig 12)

Built in 1842 by the Johnstone Estate to replace the baths on the quayside, the Royal Baths were located between two streets and had grand façades on both. This neo-Classical temple to health had engaged Ionic columns on its St Thomas Street façade and Doric ones on St Mary Street. The bathing facilities were situated on both sides of a central corridor that ran between the two streets.

(21) Site of Block House Fort, The Esplanade (*see* Fig 24)

The incongruous gap between York Buildings and Johnstone Row, in front of Chesterfield Place, is due to the Block House Fort. In 1790 it was described as being square in shape and built of stone, having embrasures for eight guns, although only five were mounted at this time. A further reminder of its existence is Blockhouse Lane, a narrow passage connecting St Mary Street and New Street.

(22) Johnstone Row, 60–5 The Esplanade

Johnstone Row, built *c* 1810, consists of a terrace of three-storied houses with basements and attics. It was possibly designed by the local architect James Hamilton, who was also responsible for Gloucester Row, Royal Crescent and the statue of George III.

Johnstone Row, 60–5 The Esplanade, and Statue House, Johnstone Row, 66–7 The Esplanade. [AA042020]

(23) Statue House, Johnstone Row, 66–7 The Esplanade

Built in *c* 1815, Statue House – formerly a pair of houses – forms the northern end of Johnstone Row and, together with 1 Coburg Place, forms an impressive entrance to the town centre. During its lifetime, Statue House has accommodated a number of facilities for visitors, including a circulating library.

(24) Statue of George III and Royal Bathing Machine, The Esplanade (*see* Fig 9)

Designed by the architect James Hamilton and John Sealy of Coade and Sealy, the Coade stone statue of the king on its giant plinth was unveiled in 1810. The traffic island on which it is situated is now also the location for a replica of the king's bathing machine.

(25) Royal Terrace, 68–84 The Esplanade (*see* Fig 20)

Built on part of the gardens of Gloucester Lodge, Royal Terrace was originally a row of 18 houses, built in two phases between 1816 and 1818. The three houses at either end were slightly higher and projected forward from the remaining 12. The southernmost house was demolished in 1929 for the widening of Westham Road.

Statue of George III, The Esplanade. [DP058189]

Former Corporation Nursery, Commercial Road. [DP055569]

(26) Former Noah's Ark Aquarium, Commercial Road (*see* Fig 54)

Set at the edge of the Swannery, at the western edge of what was Melcombe Regis Gardens, Noah's Ark was an aquarium set on a hull-shaped concrete base. Established in 1966, it later became an amusement arcade and is now a restaurant.

(27) Former Corporation Nursery, Commercial Road

Melcombe Regis Gardens was established in the 1920s between Westham Bridge and Melcombe Regis Station, on land reclaimed from Radipole Lake. Much of the site north of the bowling green has been turned into a car park, although part of the Corporation Nursery has survived and is now a tea room and garden centre.

(28) Gloucester Lodge, 85 The Esplanade and 86–9 The Esplanade (*see* Figs 8, 10, and 18)

Gloucester Lodge, later Royal Lodge, was built in 1780 for Prince William Henry, Duke of Gloucester, but was purchased by his brother, George III, in 1801. After his death the house was sold and in the third quarter of the 19th century it became the Gloucester Hotel and was extended to the south. It was severely damaged by fire in 1927, and during the subsequent rebuilding it was raised by a storey.

(29) Royal Hotel, 90–1 The Esplanade (*see* Figs 17, 18, 42 and 65)

Andrew Sproule built this hotel on waste ground to the north of Melcombe Regis in the 1770s. It included a new assembly room that superseded the early one on the south side of the harbour. The hotel was demolished in 1891 and was replaced by a new, purpose-built hotel erected between 1897 and 1899 to designs by Charles Orlando Law.

(30) Royal Arcade, 92 The Esplanade

Contemporary with the Royal Hotel, this shopping arcade with 14 shops replaced a terraced house in Gloucester Row. In 1925 one of the tenants in the arcade was an office belonging to Messrs Marsh & Wright, manufacturers and suppliers of bathing tents.

(31) Northern part of Gloucester Row, 93–9 The Esplanade (*see* Fig 65)

Probably designed by James Hamilton and erected in *c* 1790, this section of Gloucester Row was originally a terrace of eight houses, the northernmost one having been demolished in the early 20th century to widen King Street.

(32) Jubilee Memorial Clock, The Esplanade

The Memorial Clock was erected in 1887–8 to commemorate the Golden Jubilee of Queen Victoria. Built in cast and wrought iron on a stone base, the clock has four faces and each side has panels containing the queen's head and the borough's coat of arms. Inscriptions record that the memorial was erected by public subscription and that the clock was a gift from Sir Henry Edwards.

Royal Hotel, 90–1 The Esplanade. [DP055551]

Jubilee Memorial Clock, The Esplanade. [DP054495]

(33) Royal Crescent, 101–15 The Esplanade

The original intention was to construct a large crescent of 49 terraced houses to the north of Gloucester Row; however, this scheme was abandoned, though the name was retained. Royal Crescent, built *c* 1800–5 by James Hamilton, is a straight terrace of 15 houses.

(34) Belvidere, 116–31 The Esplanade (*see* Fig 22)

Belvidere was begun in 1818, though it was only completed in the early 1850s. It is a palace-fronted terrace of 16 houses, with the 2 central houses and the 2 houses at either end projecting slightly.

(35) Victoria Terrace, 132–46 The Esplanade (*see* Fig 43)

Built in 1855–6, Victoria Terrace was one of the last, palace-fronted façades using classical forms built at a seaside resort. The centrepiece of the terrace is the Prince Regent Hotel (formerly the Burdon Hotel), which projects beyond the flanking terraced houses.

(36) Pier Bandstand, The Esplanade (*see* Figs 49 and 68)

V J Wenning's scheme for the Pier Bandstand was the winning entry of 26 that were submitted to a national architectural competition. It was officially opened on 25 May 1939 and comprised a two-storey block on the Esplanade, opposite Victoria Terrace, with a performance area that could seat 2,400 projecting over the beach.

Victoria Terrace, 132–46 The Esplanade. [DP054498]

Pier Bandstand, The Esplanade. [DP055536]

(37) Round House, 1–2 Brunswick Terrace, and 3–22 Brunswick Terrace

Built between 1823 and 1827, Brunswick Terrace is the northernmost seafront terrace. Designed by Morris Clarke and George Cox, the terrace consists of 20 narrow houses, each with a bow window or a canted bay window. Round House at the southern end of the terrace, echoes the curved form of 1 Devonshire Buildings, Statue House and 1 Coburg Place.

Waterloo Place. [DP055561]

Brunswick Terrace. [DP055523]

(38) Waterloo Place

Waterloo Place is a terrace of 12 houses built in *c* 1835 at the northern end of the Esplanade, behind Brunswick Terrace.

(39) Lennox House, 47 Lennox Street

This originally detached villa of *c* 1845 is marked on Pierse Arthur's 1857 *Trigonometrical Map of Weymouth and Melcombe Regis* as Victoria Villa. The map has a label suggesting that 'Hydropathic Baths' may have been available in the villa or, more probably, were housed in a now demolished building to the rear.

Other titles in the Informed Conservation series

Behind the Veneer: The South Shoreditch furniture trade and its buildings.
Joanna Smith and Ray Rogers, 2006. Product code 51204, ISBN 9781873592960

The Birmingham Jewellery Quarter: An introduction and guide.
John Cattell and Bob Hawkins, 2000. Product code 50205, ISBN 9781850747772

Bridport and West Bay: The buildings of the flax and hemp industry.
Mike Williams, 2006. Product code 51167, ISBN 9781873592861

Building a Better Society: Liverpool's historic institutional buildings.
Colum Giles, 2008. Product code 51332, ISBN 9781873592908

Built on Commerce: Liverpool's central business district.
Joseph Sharples and John Stonard, 2008. Product code 51331, ISBN 9781905624348

Built to Last? The buildings of the Northamptonshire boot and shoe industry.
Kathryn A Morrison with Ann Bond, 2004. Product code 50921, ISBN 9781873592793

Gateshead: Architecture in a changing English urban landscape.
Simon Taylor and David Lovie, 2004. Product code 52000, ISBN 9781873592762

Manchester's Northern Quarter.
Simon Taylor and Julian Holder, 2008. Product code 50946, ISBN 9781873592847

Manchester: The warehouse legacy – An introduction and guide.
Simon Taylor, Malcolm Cooper and P S Barnwell, 2002. Product code 50668, ISBN 9781873592670

Margate's Seaside Heritage.
Nigel Barker, Allan Brodie, Nick Dermott, Lucy Jessop and Gary Winter, 2007. Product code 51335, ISBN 9781905624669

Newcastle's Grainger Town: An urban renaissance.
Fiona Cullen and David Lovie, 2003. Product code 50811, ISBN 9781873592779

'One Great Workshop': The buildings of the Sheffield metal trades.
Nicola Wray, Bob Hawkins and Colum Giles, 2001. Product code 50214, ISBN 9781873592663

Ordinary Landscapes, Special Places: Anfield, Breckfield and the growth of Liverpool's suburbs.
Adam Menuge, 2008. Product code 51343, ISBN 9781873592892

Places of Health and Amusement: Liverpool's historic parks and gardens.
Katy Layton-Jones and Robert Lee, 2008. Product code 51333, ISBN 9781873592915

Religion and Place in Leeds.
John Minnis with Trevor Mitchell, 2007. Product code 51337, ISBN 9781905624485

Religion and Place: Liverpool's historic places of worship.
Sarah Brown and Peter de Figueiredo, 2008. Product code 51334, ISBN 9781873592885

Storehouses of Empire: Liverpool's historic warehouses.
Colum Giles and Bob Hawkins, 2004. Product code 50920, ISBN 9781873592809

Stourport-on-Severn: Pioneer town of the canal age.
Colum Giles, Keith Falconer, Barry Jones and Michael Taylor, 2007. Product code 51290, ISBN 9781905624362

£7.99 each (plus postage and packing)

To order
Tel: EH Sales 01761 452966
Email: ehsales@gillards.com
Online bookshop: www.english-heritage.org.uk

Map of Weymouth showing the location of the buildings mentioned in the gazetteer

KEY

1	Nothe Fort	22	Johnstone Row
2	Former Red Barracks/Wellington Court	23	Statue House
3	Brewers Quay	24	Statue of George III and Royal Bathing Machine
4	Old Rooms Inn	25	Royal Terrace
5	Ralph Allen's House	26	Former Noah's Ark Aquarium
6	Town Bridge	27	Former Corporation Nursery
7	Former warehouse/Deep Sea Adventure	28	Gloucester Lodge
8	Site of bathhouse	29	Royal Hotel
9	Pavilion Theatre	30	Royal Arcade
10	Pier Bathing Station, Pleasure Pier	31	Gloucester Row
11	Devonshire Buildings	32	Jubilee Memorial Clock
12	Pulteney Buildings	33	Royal Crescent
13	Former sanatorium, Clarence Buildings	34	Belvidere
14	Alexandra Gardens	35	Victoria Terrace
15	Site of Theatre Royal	36	Pier Bandstand
16	Former library	37	Brunswick Terrace
17	Charlotte Row and York Buildings	38	Waterloo Place
18	Site of Jubilee Hall and Arcadia	39	Lennox House
19	Frederick Place		
20	Site of Royal Baths		
21	Site of Block House Fort		